DATE DUE	

I want to be a Builder

I WANT TO BE A
Builder

DAN LIEBMAN

FIREFLY BOOKS

A FIREFLY BOOK

Published by Firefly Books Ltd. 2003

First Printing

Publisher Cataloging-in-Publication Data (U.S.)
(Library of Congress Standards)

Liebman, Dan.
   I want to be a builder/ Dan Liebman. —1st ed.
[24] p. : col. photos. ; cm. (I want to be)
Summary: Photographs and easy-to-read text describe the job of a builder.
ISBN 1-55297-758-7
ISBN 1-55297-757-9 (pbk.)
1. Building trades – Vocational guidance – Juvenile literature. (1. Building trades – Vocational guidance. 2. Vocational guidance.) I. Title. II. Series.
624/.023 21   TH159.L54 2003

Published in the United States in 2003 by
Firefly Books (U.S.) Inc.
P.O. Box 1338, Ellicott Station
Buffalo, New York, USA., 14205

National Library of Canada Cataloguing in
Publication Data

Liebman, Daniel
   I want to be a builder / Dan Liebman.

ISBN 1-55297-758-7 (bound)
ISBN 1-55297-757-9 (pbk.)

1. Building – Vocational guidance – Juvenile literature.
I. Title.

TH159.L53 2003   624'.023   C2003-902828-3

Published in Canada in 2003 by
Firefly Books Ltd.
3680 Victoria Park Avenue
Toronto, Ontario, Canada, M2H 3K1

Photo Credits

© Al Harvey/Slide Farm, pages 8, 15, 17
© Laura Zito, page 9
© MediaFocus International, LLC, pages 10, 11
© PhotoDisc/Ryan McVay, page 12, front cover
© Mark E. Gibson Stock Photography, page 21,
© B. Allan Mackie, page 23
© George Walker/Firefly Books, pages 5, 6–7, 13,
   14, 16, 18, 19, 20, 22, 24, back cover

The author and publisher would like to thank:

Morah Duclos
Massimo Ighani
Trevor Trottier
Dylan Walker
Nicholas Walker

Design by Interrobang Graphic Design Inc.
Printed and bound in Canada by Friesens, Altona, Manitoba

The Publisher acknowledges the financial support of the Government of Canada through the Book Publishing Industry Development Program for its publishing activities.

Builders like putting things together.

They build houses, apartment buildings and office buildings.

Some builders work high above the ground.

Builders don't only build buildings. These builders are putting up a bridge. Other builders build highways.

Building a log house requires special skills. These men are putting up the roof.

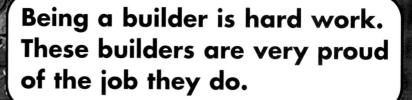

Being a builder is hard work. These builders are very proud of the job they do.